Published by Creative Education
P.O. Box 227, Mankato, Minnesota 56002
Creative Education is an imprint of The Creative Company

Design by Stephanie Blumenthal; Production by The Design Lab
Printed in the United States of America

Photographs by Andrew Bannister, Robert E. Barber, Steven Burkule, CLEO Photography,
Corbis (Nathan Benn), Dennis Frates, Getty Images (AFP), Don Geyer, The Image Finders (Jim
Barron, Patty McConville), JLM Visuals (Richard P. Jacobs, Breck P. Kent, Lowell R. Laudon),
George Robbins, Tom Stack & Associates (Sharon Gerig, Thomas Kitchin, Brian Parker, Doug
Sokell, Therisa Stack, Tom Stack, Spencer Swanger, TSADO/NASA, Greg Vaughn)

Library of Congress Cataloging-in-Publication Data
Frisch, Aaron.
Rivers / by Aaron Frisch.
p. cm. — (Our world)
Includes index.
ISBN 978-1-58341-573-3
1. Stream ecology—Juvenile literature. 2. Rivers—Juvenile literature. I. Title
QH541.5.S7F75 2008   577.6'4—dc22   2006102991

First edition
2 4 6 8 9 7 5 3 1

OUR WORLD

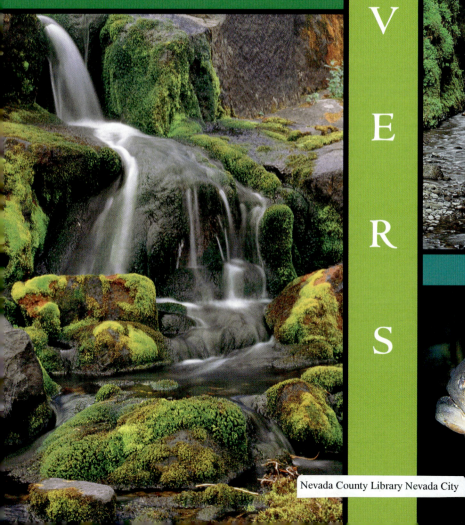

R
I
V
E
R
S

Aaron Frisch

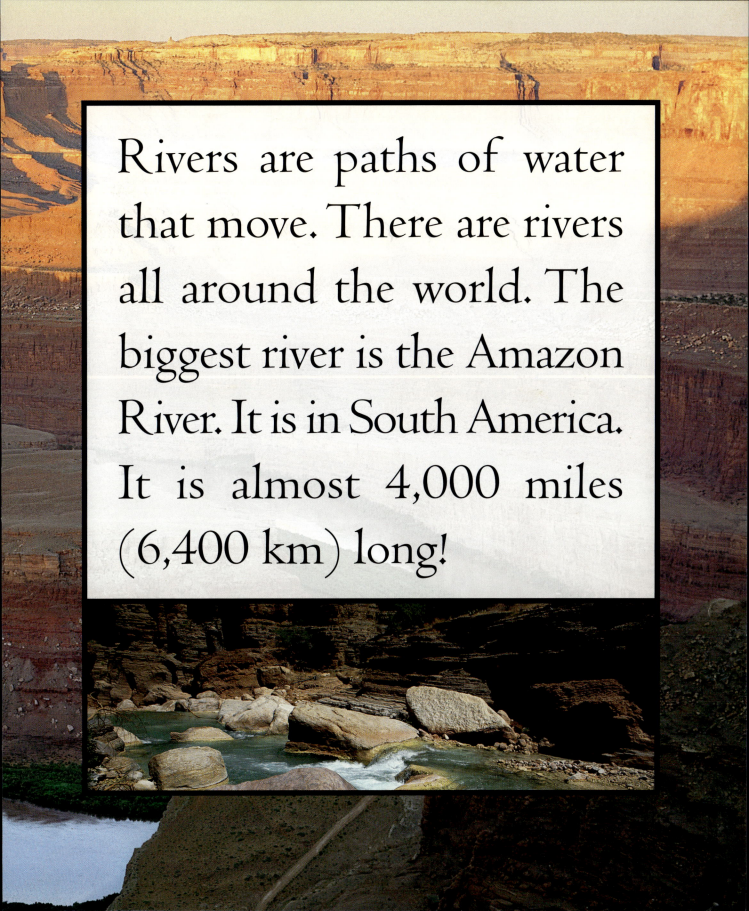

Rivers are paths of water that move. There are rivers all around the world. The biggest river is the Amazon River. It is in South America. It is almost 4,000 miles (6,400 km) long!

Rivers get water in different ways. Water from rain and snow go into them. There is lots of water underneath the ground. It is called groundwater. It comes up and goes into rivers.

Snow melts and goes into rivers

Most big rivers get water from little rivers. Little rivers run into the big rivers. A river that adds water to a bigger river is called a tributary (*TRIB-yoo-tare-ee*). Many big rivers flow to the ocean.

Lots of rivers end
in the ocean

Sometimes rivers get too much water. They flow over their **banks**. This is called a flood. Floods can hurt houses and roads.

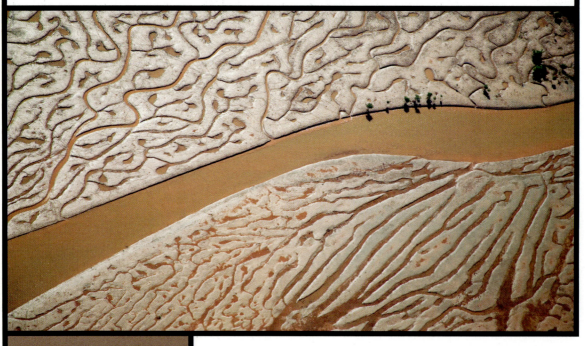

Floods can make rivers go over roads

Rivers can change the land. When water flows over the land, it cuts into the ground. This takes a very long time. Canyons (*CAN-yuns*) are places where rivers have cut deep into the ground.

Rivers can make deep canyons

Some rivers have pretty waterfalls

Some rivers move fast. Other rivers move slowly. Fast river water is called rapids. Many canyons have rapids. Some rivers have **waterfalls**. Big waterfalls make **mist** go into the air.

Lots of animals live in rivers. Fish and frogs live in rivers. So do some crabs. Ducks swim on rivers. Big animals like bears catch fish in rivers. Most rivers have plants like weeds in them, too.

Fish and other animals live in rivers

People use rivers for different things. Farmers use river water to help their **crops** grow. People can ride in boats on rivers. People get water for drinking from rivers. Sometimes people build **dams** on rivers. Dams make it easier to use the water.

Water goes to farm fields and over dams

People and animals need rivers. But many rivers are polluted *(puh-LOO-ted)*. This means they are dirty and not healthy. People should not put garbage into rivers. Then rivers will be clean and pretty for a long time!

*People use big boats
on many rivers*

Find a little hill of sand or dirt. Use your finger to make a groove in it. Make the groove go from the top to the bottom. Make it go back and forth. Slowly pour a big glass of water into the groove at the top. The water will flow down like a river. What happens if you block the river?

GLOSSARY

banks—the ground along the sides of a river

crops—the plants that a farmer grows

dams—walls that people build to block or change rivers

mist—tiny drops of water that look like a cloud

waterfalls—places where a river flows from higher ground to lower ground

LEARN MORE ABOUT RIVERS

BBC Schools
http://www.bbc.co.uk/schools/riversandcoasts/index.shtml
This site is like taking a field trip to a river.

Missouri Botanical Garden
http://www.mbgnet.net/fresh/rivers/index.htm
This site has all kinds of facts about rivers.